ST. ANTHONY OF PADUA
Our Franciscan Friend

FRANCIS OF ASSISI BLESSES
ANTHONY OF PADUA.

ST. ANTHONY OF PADUA

Our Franciscan Friend

Guidelines, Devotions and Prayers
for Growth in the Spirit of
St. Anthony of Padua

Illustrated

CATHOLIC BOOK PUBLISHING CO.
New York

IMPRIMI POTEST: Anthony M. Carrozzo, O.F.M.
Provincial Minister, Franciscan Holy Name Province

NIHIL OBSTAT: James T. O'Connor, S.T.D.
Censor Librorum

IMPRIMATUR: ✠ Patrick J. Sheridan, D.D.
Vicar General, Archdiocese of New York

Revised Edition, 1991
Editorial Ministry: Rev. Cassian A. Miles, O.F.M. and Janet E. Gianopoulos

For acknowledgments, see p. 127

(T-110)

CONTENTS

FOREWORD

AS friends of St. Anthony, you and I belong to a great community or communion of saints. In our Eucharistic gatherings we hear the celebrant pray, "From age to age you gather a people to yourself." Yes, all of us are destined to "share eternal life with Mary, the Virgin Mother of God, with the apostles and with all the saints who have done your will throughout the ages." We ask God to "remember your Church throughout the world," "the entire people your Son has gained for you," and "accept this offering from your whole family."

What the Church is telling us is that we belong to a community which includes the Blessed Mother and Peter and Paul and Francis of Assisi and Clare and St. Anthony of Padua. I like to think of the community or communion of saints as a great circle of people with hands joined, praying. Many of the people are visible, but many are not—they have gone on, into eternity. But their hands are joined to ours.

It is a long-standing Christian tradition that the saints in heaven pray for us on earth, and we in turn honor them for the great gifts God has given them and ask them for their help and prayers.

You and I have a special friend in St. Anthony of Padua (1195-1231). A contemporary of St. Francis of Assisi, Anthony, like ourselves, wanted to live for something beyond himself that would give meaning to his life. As a young Augustinian in Portugal, he was so inspired by the martyrdom of five Franciscan friars in Morocco that he became a Franciscan. He soon became a well-known preacher, proclaiming the Gospel through France and Italy, where large crowds filled town squares and vast fields to hear his sermons. Anthony was able to call people to a deeper faith because he himself was a man of faith. He never lost sight of the transcendent dimension of his own life which enabled others to see in him the transcendent dimension of their lives. He was truly a living Gospel to others. And that's what makes Anthony a Wonder Worker, a friend to all of us.

I pray that through the prayers and devotions in this prayer book, and through the intercession of St. Anthony of Padua, we may become ever more deeply aware of God's faithful love and indwelling presence—and, at the end of our earthly pilgrimage, share fully in the deep and intimate oneness of the Triune God.

Rev. Kevin E. Mackin, O.F.M.
Director of St. Anthony's Guild

GETTING
TO KNOW
ST. ANTHONY

"Let all people contemplate St. Anthony, this light of sanctity, in which the Catholic Church glories. Let them form their lives after his deeds and virtues."

—*Pope Pius XI*

"Each saint in heaven rejoices over the glorification of the others, and each saint's love overflows to the others. . . .

"The same joy will fill all the blessed, for I shall rejoice over your well-being as though it were my own, and you will rejoice over mine as though it were yours.

"To use an example: See, we are standing together, and I have a rose in my hand. The rose is mine, and yet you no less than I rejoice in its beauty and its perfume. So shall it be in eternal life: My glory shall be your consolation and exultation, and yours shall be mine."

—Sermons of St. Anthony of Padua

Saint of the Whole World

ST. Anthony of Padua is the name by which he is generally known. He was only a young man when he died. Padua was indeed his last home on earth. His relics rest there today, honored by thousands every year in a basilica built in his honor.

Since his death and by his intercession, countless miracles have been reported through more than seven centuries in all parts of the world.

But Padua, in northern Italy, was not his native city. Anthony was born in Lisbon, Portugal, in 1195, according to tradition on the feast of Mary's Assumption. A contemporary of St. Francis of Assisi, he was to become his most illustrious disciple.

The fact is that neither the people of Italy nor the people of Portugal can claim him exclusively as their own. St. Anthony is the Saint of the Whole World—a universal saint for a universal Church. Like Mother Teresa today, he was one who followed Francis as an instrument of peace in caring about people.

Devotion to St. Anthony and the Franciscans forms a part of life in nearly every land. Visit a Catholic church of any size and you will most likely find a statue or stained glass window of St. Anthony and a Way of the Cross—popularized by the Franciscans.

See also the Chronology on pp. 119-121.

Wherever you go, you will find Christians praying to St. Anthony about the troubles and challenges in their daily lives—especially to find things they have lost.

The Young Augustinian

FERNANDO (Ferdinand in English) was the Saint's baptismal name. Born of an aristocratic family, he was probably about 15 years old when he said farewell to the bright worldly prospects that lay before him. Fernando consecrated himself in about 1210 to the service of God as a religious among the Canons Regular of St. Augustine.

But in the Augustinian monastery near his native city he was distracted by visits from relatives and friends. After spending two years there, he asked to be transferred to another monastery. He was sent to Holy Cross in Coimbra, a great center of learning and the capital of Portugal at that time.

Fernando devoted the next eight years of his life to study and prayer, immersing himself in Sacred Scripture. This period laid the foundation for his later work of preaching the Gospel.

At Olivais, near his monastery, a few early followers of St. Francis had a little dwelling. Fernando often helped them when they begged for alms. He admired the humble, joyful hearts of these men who cheerfully renounced worldly values. But a far greater sacrifice by these zealous Franciscans proved the turning point in Fernando's idealistic life.

Follower of St. Francis

IN 1219 St. Francis had sent his first missionaries—Berard, Peter, Accursio, Adiuto and Otto—to the Muslims. When they urged that the king of Morocco convert to the Christian faith, he put them to death by the sword on January 16, 1220. The relics of these friars were brought back to Portugal and laid to rest in the church of the Holy Cross in Coimbra where Fernando lived.

Inspired by the friars' martyrdom, he felt called to join the Franciscans and give his life for Christ preaching the Gospel to the Muslims. He joined the Franciscan community at Olivais in the summer of 1220, taking the name of Anthony, a saintly hermit of the fourth century.

He then set sail for Morocco, but on reaching his destination fell seriously ill and was bedridden for several months. Forced to abandon his plans, he decided to return home. En route, his ship encountered a severe storm and was driven to the coast of Sicily, south of Messina, where Franciscan friars welcomed him and nursed him to health.

In the spring of 1221, a general gathering of some 3,000 Franciscans took place at Assisi, and Anthony went to meet his new brothers. Afterward, seeking God's will, he spent a year in Montepaolo at a mountain hermitage of the frairs. Invoking the heritage of his patron saint, he devoted himself to prayer and study in the daily life of a hermit.

Preacher of God's Love

GOD'S call to Anthony to enter into the heart of the world came in the summer of 1222. After a priestly ordination of Franciscans and Dominicans at Forli, all gathered for a festive dinner. When no one accepted the superior's invitation to give a talk, he called on Anthony. The friars were soon spellbound by his words—awed by his knowledge of the Scriptures and moved by his eloquence and fervor.

Soon afterward Anthony embarked on his career as a Franciscan preacher that would continue through France and Italy for the next nine years. His sermons often drew large crowds that overflowed town squares and filled vast fields.

The Franciscan final Rule was approved by Pope Honorious III in 1223. Around the same time, Anthony was chosen by Francis to teach theology to his friars, uniting the vision of St. Augustine with the ideals of Francis.

This became the special mark of the Franciscan school of theology. Anthony also served as leader of the Franciscans in a region of northern Italy.

St. Francis died in 1226 and was canonized in 1228. From that year onward Anthony took a residence in Padua but was often on the road, continuing a lasting Franciscan mission of love at work. In his sermons, he defended the Church's teachings against those who rejected them. He spoke out against unjust interest rates and interceded for debtors. He challenged people to give alms to the poor. His stirring words revealed how deeply he understood the problems of the people.

And he strengthened his words with a holy life. "The preacher must by word and example," he wrote, "be a sun to those to whom he preaches. You are, says the Lord, the light of the world . . . our light must warm the hearts of people, while our teaching enlightens them."

Perhaps one of the most famous stories about the Saint concerns an appearance of Jesus to him in the form of a child near the end of Anthony's life. He was working on a book of sermons for saints' feasts, while staying at a small Franciscan friary not far from Padua. Anthony's mystical experience of the Child Jesus reflects the central place of the Incarnation of the Son of God in his sermons.

After giving a series of Lenten sermons to the people of Padua in the spring of 1231, Anthony became seriously ill. In the chaplain's quarters of the Poor Clare Convent at Arcella near Padua, on June 13, 1231, he died singing, like St. Francis—his final song, a hymn to Mary.

The children of Padua ran through the streets calling out, "The Saint has died! The holy father has died!"

The Gospel Doctor

THE Church declared Anthony a saint on May 30, 1232, less than a year after his death. Construction of a worthy burial-church was soon underway for him in Padua. When Anthony's remains were transferred to the newly completed basilica in 1263, his tongue was found intact. Reverence for the Saint spread from his burial place and has continued ever since.

Anthony's knowledge of the Scriptures is reflected in his "Sunday Sermons." A collection of materials to help preachers compose their own talks, these sermons were written in Padua about 1228. Because these texts interwove Anthony's glowing brand of Franciscan spirituality with enduring verses from the Gospel, on January 16, 1946, Pope Pius

XII proclaimed him "worthy of the title 'Doctor of the Gospel'. . . a Doctor of the Universal Church." This means that the Church recognizes him as a wise teacher of the Gospel of Jesus Christ, even today.

Images of Anthony

UNDOUBTEDLY, St. Anthony worked many miracles during his lifetime—particularly on behalf of the sick. But he truly became the Wonder Worker of Padua after his death. His fame in obtaining miraculous favors from God has inspired artists throughout the ages. Many images have come to be associated with him as a consequence of this influence—the Child Jesus on his arm, the Bible or a lily in his hand, a loaf of bread extended to the poor.

Anthony's reputation as a "finder of lost things" assures us that evil cannot overwhelm us, for we have been redeemed by Christ—and that no request is too small for us to make of our heavenly friends, the saints.

Contemporary devotion also invokes Anthony as a "finder of lost faith" for those alienated from the Church and as a healer of emotional problems as well as bodily sufferings.

"Through Anthony to Jesus"

PER Antonium ad Jesum (Through Anthony to Jesus) were the memorable words that Pope Pius XI used in encouraging the faithful to practice devotion to the Saint of Padua. To nurture that form of Franciscan spirituality has been the aim of this little guide since St. Anthony's Guild first published it in 1928 as *St. Anthony's Treasury.*

This revised edition includes a collection of quotations from Anthony's sermons and traditional prayers to him as well as contemporary ones—particularly for the increasing celebrations of Tuesday devotions to St. Anthony. A special section offers guidance for living in the spirit of the Saint.

Through these pages may today's followers of St. Anthony of Padua enjoy their times of prayer, live their faith with love, and become instruments of that faith in the world.

The Wisdom of
St. Anthony

(Selected from the Sermons of St. Anthony.)

JESUS' place should always be in the center of every heart. From this center, as if from a sun, emanate rays of grace to each of us.

✠   ✠   ✠

WHO can be more blessed or happier than one in whom God has set up his dwelling place? What else can you need or what else can possibly make you richer? You have everything when you have within you the One who made all things, the only One who can satisfy the longings of your spirit, without whom everything else is nothing.

✠   ✠   ✠

WHAT a superabundance of love, zeal, and joy a soul experiences when it possesses God! Superabundant love elevates the soul beyond its limited confines; enthusiasm and zeal for God motivate the soul beyond its capacities; joy frees it from all sadness.

✠   ✠   ✠

D O you want to have everything? Give all of yourself and God will give you all of himself, and thus, not having anything of yourself, you will totally possess God and yourself in him.

✠   ✠   ✠

A vessel is hollow, able to contain any-thing that is poured into it. It is a fitting symbol of humility, a virtue that makes a person receptive to the infusion of divine grace.

✠   ✠   ✠

T HE earth represents the body of Christ. Just as the earth, plowed and broken in springtime, produces abundant fruit at harvest time, so the bruised and broken body of Christ merited for us the harvest of the heavenly Kingdom. The Body of Christ, the Church, germinated with the apostles, flowed in the sacrifice of the martyrs, and yielded abundant fruit in its believers.

✠   ✠   ✠

THE altar on the earth is symbolic of the human nature of Jesus Christ. The altar in heaven is a symbol of the Trinity. The altar within us is a symbol of the inner holiness of the heart.

✠　　✠　　✠

WE need external peace to live with others, internal peace to live with ourselves and eternal peace to live with God.

✠　　✠　　✠

THE image of God in human beings, deformed and obscured by sin, was restored and illumined by the Holy Spirit, who breathed the breath of life into them.

✠　　✠　　✠

MAY your love grow in knowledge and understanding, so that you may know how to discern not only between good and evil but also between what is good and what is even better.

✠　　✠　　✠

IF you offend or hurt Christ by sinning grievously, as soon as you offer him a flower of regret or a rose of sincere confession, he immediately forgets your offenses, forgives you your sins, and hurries to embrace and kiss you.

✠   ✠   ✠

JESUS, sweet name, enhancing name! A name that is a joyful cry for the heart, that is music to the ear and honey in the mouth! A name that comforts sinners and offers blessed hope.

✠   ✠   ✠

THE love of God will make us hate sin. The things of this earth will lose their attraction for us. We will find our delight in the contemplation not of this earth but of heaven.

✠   ✠   ✠

TRULY honest persons possess a harmonious and pleasant demeanor: nothing reproachable can be found in their actions, nothing inappropriate in their words, nothing indecent in their manner. Being spontaneous and respectful, their behavior wins the admiration and goodwill of all.

ONLY righteous persons walk the way faithfully and humbly, turning neither to the right, to avoid burdening themselves with worldly goods, nor to the left, so as not to fall into adversity. They follow it faithfully until they enter into the promised land.

CHRIST is our life in example, truth in promise, life in reward; a way that is straight, a truth that does not deceive, a life that never ends.

ONLY if we keep in our hearts the memory of Christ's wounds and listen to his words will we find true peace in our hearts.

LET us ask and humbly implore the mercy of Jesus Christ, that he may come among us with his gift of peace; that he may take away all doubt from our hearts; that he may instill in our souls a strong faith in the passion and resurrection, so that we may merit to receive eternal life with the apostles and with the faithful of the Church.

✠   ✠   ✠

WE ask you, our Lady, Mother of God, exalted above the choirs of angels, that you fill the vessel of our hearts with grace; that you make it shine with the gold of wisdom; that you make it resolute with the power of your virtue; that you adorn it with the precious stones of virtue.

✠   ✠   ✠

WE ask you, Lord, allow us to come to the wedding feast of your Incarnation with faith and humility; to celebrate the wedding feast of penance, which will make us worthy to attend the wedding feast of heavenly glory.

✠   ✠   ✠

LOVE is essential, so that without love all our efforts are in vain, no matter how much good we accomplish.

✠   ✠   ✠

WITH love in our hearts, we will approach God with humility, others with compassion, and ourselves with respectful purity.

✠   ✠   ✠

LOVE prompts us to forgive our brothers and sisters who wrong us. Love helps us to correct our erring brothers and sisters. Love makes us compassionate and caring.

✠   ✠   ✠

SEEK God's Kingdom above all else. Make it the most important thing in your life. Everything else must be sought in view of this Kingdom; nothing should be asked beyond it. Whatever we ask must serve this end.

✠   ✠   ✠

THE compassion of God is without limits or measure; it is incomprehensible to our finite intelligence. God's compassion embraces and includes all.

✠   ✠   ✠

COMPASSION toward our neighbors ought to be threefold: if they sin against us, we ought to forgive them. If they stray from the path of rectitude and truth, we should instruct them. If they are in need, we must help them.

✠   ✠   ✠

LET us ask Jesus Christ, our Lord, to fill us with his mercy, so that we may practice compassion with ourselves and others, not judging nor condemning them, but forgiving those who hurt us and helping those who are in need.

✠   ✠   ✠

THOSE who open their mouth to confess their faith breathe the spirit of divine grace, which is the life of the soul. Christ the

Lord is our very breath when we openly proclaim with our mouths what we believe with our hearts. And, if it is sweet to pronounce his name now, how much sweeter will it be when we enjoy fully the glory of his Kingdom.

✠ ✠ ✠

LET us ask our Lord, who has clothed himself with the "coarse sackcloth" of our humanity at his first coming, to wake us up so that we may merit the gift of eternal salvation at his last coming.

✠ ✠ ✠

HE who is the beginning and the end, the ruler of the angels, made himself obedient to human creatures. The creator of the heavens obeys a carpenter; the God of eternal glory listens to a poor virgin. Has anyone ever witnessed anything comparable to this? Has any ear heard anything like this? Let the philosopher no longer disdain from listening to the common laborer; the wise to the simple; the educated, to the illiterate; a child of a prince, to a peasant.

✠ ✠ ✠

St. Anthony's Friends

"It is not enough that you love St. Anthony," Pope Leo XIII reminded us, *"but you must make him loved."*

WE all wish to have St. Anthony as our heavenly friend and to share in his protection. How can we become more devoted to him?

Tell others about your devotion to St. Anthony.

● Point out the specific ways in which St. Anthony has helped you.

● Invite others to accompany you to church for the novena service to St. Anthony.

● Suggest that your parish provide a novena each Tuesday if none is available.

● Show this book to your relatives, neighbors, coworkers and friends to encourage their own devotion to the Saint.

● Offer a gift membership in St. Anthony's Guild.

Include St. Anthony in your daily spiritual life. Use his assistance.

● Honor the Saint by praying the Responsory of St. Anthony, his Litany or other prayers from this book. Say the Chaplet of

St. Anthony (see page 62). Keep a picture of St. Anthony in your home or place of work, in your handbag or wallet. Wear a medal with his image. Visit his shrine in your church and light a candle.

• Each Tuesday go to the St. Anthony novena service in your church or, if none is available, make your own private novena. Make the "Thirteen Tuesdays" to prepare for the feast of St. Anthony on June 13. Make the Nine Tuesdays to get ready for Christmas.

• Try to imitate St. Anthony's virtues, particularly his love for the Word of God, by reading a little from the Bible each day. Take part in Mass and receive Holy Communion when you can. Reach out to the needy and lonely, the homeless or people in nursing homes. Volunteer your time or talents to your parish and local service organizations.

Honor St. Anthony by joining his Guild, supporting the good works of the Franciscans.

• As a young Franciscan friar, Fr. John Forest Loviner, O.F.M., heard many inspiring stories about favors that people had received by praying to St. Anthony of Padua. Fr. John dreamed of bringing these friends together in Anthony's honor, as Pope Leo had observed. Thus was born, in Paterson, N.J., the family known today as St. Anthony's Guild.

● From 1930 to 1970, the publishing activities of the Guild included the development of *The New American Bible* and religious educational materials for the Confraternity of Christian Doctrine.

● The members of the Guild have supported, prayed for and followed with interest the education and good works of the Franciscan friars of Holy Name Province, particularly those on behalf of the poor. If you would like more information, write to The Franciscans, St. Anthony's Guild, Paterson, NJ 07509-2948.

HONORING
ST. ANTHONY

"It is pious and just that those whom God crowns and honors in heaven because of their merit and holiness we should honor and glorify on earth by our prayers and veneration."   —*Pope Gregory IX*

Tuesday, St. Anthony's Day

GOD called St. Anthony to eternal life on June 13, 1231. The Saint had wanted to be laid to rest at home in Padua. But when the news spread of his death, disputes arose over the possession of the remains of this extraordinarily popular Franciscan, just as had happened with Francis himself.

The following Tuesday, Anthony's remains were finally borne in a triumphal funeral procession to the friars' church in Padua. The day saw a marvelous manifestation of favors granted to all who called on the Saint for his intercession.

As a result, Tuesday became particularly associated with St. Anthony. Down through the centuries, pilgrims to his tomb have gathered there on Tuesdays to pray for their needs.

Tradition claims that in the year 1617 Tuesday became securely established as St. Anthony's Day by the Saint himself. A noblewoman who lived in Bologna in Italy had prayed before his altar for the gift of a child after 22 years of marriage. That night, St. Anthony appeared to her in a vision.

He instructed her to visit his statue in the church of the Friars Minor for nine consecutive Tuesdays and promised her prayers would be heard. The woman faithfully did as directed, and a child was born—but terribly deformed. Undaunted, the mother carried the baby to church, placed it on the Saint's altar, and soon afterward found the child to be in perfect health.

The story of this miracle spread rapidly throughout Italy, and the novena of Tuesdays in honor of St. Anthony became a favorite devotion. It then traveled to other countries.

Not satisfied with nine Tuesdays, the faithful increased the number to 13 to commemorate the day on which the Saint had died. The Church has encouraged these special Tuesday prayers in honor of St. Anthony.

"St. Anthony's Bread"

ST. Anthony is today, as he was in his lifetime, the faithful friend of all in trouble, especially the poor and the needy. "St. Anthony's Bread" means that when a person prays to the Saint for a favor, he or she promises to give a gift ("bread") to the poor or some charitable cause.

This custom goes back to the year 1888. At that time there lived in Toulon, France, a devout young woman named Louise Bouffier, who managed a small bakery store.

One morning Louise couldn't open the door with her key. Neither could a locksmith, who told her he would have to break the door open. While he went to get his tools, Louise promised St. Anthony she would give some bread to the poor if the door could be opened without force. When the locksmith returned, she begged him to try just once more. The door opened.

Louise kept her promise and the poor received their bread. This answer to Louise's prayers became known to her friends, and they began to imitate her example. One of them bought a little statue of St. Anthony and placed it in the back room of the shop. It soon became a well-known shrine.

From Toulon this devotion spread to all parts of the world. Sometimes travelers going on a long voyage would promise an offering in bread to St. Anthony if they made their journey safely. Sometimes a mother asked for the health of her sick child. A family might ask for the conversion of someone who was dying and refused to see a priest. All those petitions accompanied by a promise of bread were granted.

Pope Leo XIII, in his letter of 1898 on the Thirteen Tuesdays, commended the practice of giving "St. Anthony's Bread" to the needy.

A Prayer of Thanksgiving before Giving "St. Anthony's Bread"

GLORIOUS St. Anthony, friend of the poor and comforter of the troubled, you have come with loving care to my assistance. To express my heartfelt thanks, I ask you to accept this offering with my sincere promise to live always in the love of Jesus and my neighbor. Continue to shield me with your protection. Obtain for me the final grace of entering one day into the kingdom of heaven, to sing with you the everlasting praises of God. Amen.

Blessing "St. Anthony's Bread"

(The public blessing is customary in churches where breads are distributed on the feast of St. Anthony, June 13, as a reminder of his charity to the poor.)

HEAVENLY Father, we praise you and give you glory for the gift of bread, fruit of the earth, work of human hands, and source of our daily nourishment. Bless this bread in honor of St. Anthony. Teach us to share the gifts you give us with the poor, the hungry, and the forsaken. Praise be to you through Jesus Christ, our Savior, in the unity of the Holy Spirit, one God forever and ever. Amen.

Table Prayers in Honor of St. Anthony

Before Meals:

FATHER, you filled St. Anthony of Padua with a great love for the needy. By feeding the poor he gave glory to your name. May we be thankful for the food on this table and reach out generously whenever we find others in need. We ask this through Christ our Lord. Amen.

After Meals:

FATHER, St. Anthony gave bread to the poor and proclaimed your glorious name. As we offer you thanks for this meal, may we be inspired to feed the hungry in the spirit of the Gospel life that St. Anthony lived so faithfully. May you be praised now and forever. Amen.

St. Anthony's Lilies

PICTURES and statues of St. Anthony often portray him holding a lily. This beautiful flower has long been regarded in Christian art as a symbol of integrity of life. In many parts of the world, lilies are in bloom in the middle of June, when the feast of St. Anthony is observed.

The custom of associating the lily with St. Anthony is related to two incidents within the last 300 years.

On the Saint's feast in 1680, a cut lily had been placed in one of the hands of his statue in the church at Mentosca d'Agesco in Austria. For a whole year the flower retained its freshness and fragrance. The following year the stalk bore two more lilies, and the church was filled with their fragrance.

Another unusual event took place on the island of Corsica at the time of the French Revolution. The Franciscans had been forced to leave the island, but the people continued to honor St. Anthony and invoke his aid, as the friars had taught them. On his feast day the people placed a shrine of the Saint and bouquets of lilies in the deserted church. Many months later, lilies placed before Anthony's statue were found still fresh and white.

Permission to bless lilies in honor of St. Anthony was given by Pope Leo XIII. Many favors have been claimed through Anthony's intercession, after applying the blessed flower petals to the sick. Like blessed palms, these lilies remain sacramentals even after they fade or are dried.

What is known as "St. Anthony's Oil" is another form of the devotion of St. Anthony's Lilies. The oil is obtained by pressing the blessed lilies.

Blessing of St. Anthony's Lilies

(The public blessing is customary on the feast of St. Anthony, June 13. Otherwise, to obtain this sacramental, an individual may request a priest to bless a lily plant in honor of St. Anthony.)

Scripture Reading

LEARN from the way the wild flowers grow. . . . If God so clothes the grass of the field, will he not much more provide for you? So do not worry and say "What are we to eat" or "What are we to wear." Your heavenly Father knows that you need them all. But seek first the kingdom of God, and his righteousness, and all these things will be given you (Matthew 6:28-33).

Prayer

FATHER, you take care of the wild flowers that neither work nor sew. You bestow spiritual gifts upon your faithful ones and reward their fidelity with eternal salvation.

Bless these lilies in honor of St. Anthony. Grant health of mind and body, holiness, happiness, and peace to those who receive these blessed lilies and who seek to observe the Gospel values of your Son, who lives and reigns with you forever. Amen.

"St. Anthony Guide" Stamps

TO facilitate the safe delivery of mail, a custom has been handed down of marking the letters "S.A.G." somewhere on a letter or package. These initials stand for "St. Anthony Guide." This brief prayer dates to an incident in July 1729.

A merchant, Don Antonio Danta, had sailed from his home in Spain for Peru many months before. As time passed, his wife, Frances, found that her funds to live on were nearly gone. In desperation she had written her husband several letters but received no reply.

One day she prayed in the Franciscan church at Oviedo. In a gesture of faith, she placed a letter for her husband in the wide sleeve of the Saint's statue and prayed for St. Anthony to guide it to her husband, trusting St. Anthony would somehow deliver it.

On returning to the statue the next morning, Frances was amazed to find not her own letter but one from her husband. Lodged in the sleeve was a heavy pouch containing 300 pesos, also sent by him.

His letter had been written shortly before in Lima, Peru, July 23, 1729. The merchant advised his wife that a letter from her had been delivered "by a friar of the Order of

St. Francis." Don Antonio was sending his reply through the same friar. To this day, the merchant's letter in Spanish is preserved in the church at Oviedo.

The story of this event soon spread throughout Spain and led to the custom of praying to St. Anthony to protect mail and give it safe passage. To signify this intent, the letters S.A.G. were placed on the mail.

Continuing this custom today, St. Anthony's Guild offers packets of stamps imprinted with S.A.G and color pictures of the Saint. If you would like to use these stamps, write to The Franciscans, St. Anthony's Guild, Paterson, N.J. 07509-2948.

Prayer Before Mailing a Letter

ST. Anthony, Guide this letter safely on its way to accomplish all I intend according to God's holy will. Amen.

PRAYERS

*"To Brother Anthony, my bishop, I,
Brother Francis, send greetings. It pleases
me that you should teach sacred theology
to the friars provided that through this
study they do not extinguish the spirit of
holy prayer and devotion, as is contained
in the Rule."* —*St. Francis of Assisi*

Introduction to Prayer

PEOPLE of all times and cultures have lifted their hearts to their Maker in prayer. Even birds and other creatures were invited by Francis of Assisi to "give praise to the Lord" who had created them.

Prayer is simply turning our attention to God. We may use words—our own, those from the Bible, or words of others. Sometimes we simply want to rest in contemplative wonder before God.

In expressing our relationship with God in prayer, we may find ourselves disposed to adoration, praise, thanksgiving, sorrow or petition. The following prayers represent these attitudes in various ways. As pathways to God, the prayers reflect our union of heart with one of the saints, Anthony of Padua.

A Journey with St. Anthony along the Way of the Cross

The Franciscans popularized the Way of the Cross devotion. In the 1300s, in their European monasteries, they began to erect Stations honoring events in the Passion of Jesus. The practice quickly spread to parish churches. By the eighteenth century the Way of the Cross had become one of the most popular devotions in the Church.

This devotion can be contemplated in churches with Stations of the Cross by walking to each Station and reflecting on the scene, or meditating on the scenes privately.

Opening Prayer

LORD Jesus, you instituted a new covenant of friendship in your blood by calling us together as the people of God. Like you, we must walk the way of the Cross.

We agonize now in the flesh to finish the remainder of your sufferings for the sake of your Body, the Church. We hasten forward to resurrection in the strength that comes from hope.

May our Lady of Sorrows walk with us now in our contemplation. Amen.

First Station
Jesus Is Condemned to Death

FOR proclaiming a Kingdom that challenges the order of his day, Jesus is condemned to die. In reality, we know it is Jesus who stands in judgment over Pilate and over our lives as well. Our Lord's love and commitment to the mission described in Isaiah "to bring glad tidings to the poor . . . to let the oppressed go free" is the true standard for judging success.

St. Anthony, help us to be fearless of the world's judgment, knowing that only the judgment of God matters.

Second Station
Jesus Accepts His Cross

WE hear Jesus' call to carry a cross and follow him. Our cross may be sickness or aging, death or separation. It may be sitting up with a sick child or listening to someone's troubles. Sharing with the poor is a special way we help take up the cross of Jesus today. In loving fidelity to God's plan, we accept our cross.

St. Anthony, help us to accept our trials for the love of God knowing that if carried in the spirit of Jesus they will also be redemptive.

Third Station
Jesus Falls the First Time

NOW the "God-man" fully tastes the frailty and poverty of the human condition. He shares the burden of those who are oppressed by human limitations. Like Jesus, we recognize our inner poverty, our vulnerability to sickness or depression or compulsive behavior. We learn from our Lord that we can embrace our human weakness, for God will be there to support us.

St. Anthony, let us be grateful to God who saves us through the cross of his beloved Son.

Fourth Station
Jesus Meets His Sorrowful Mother

EVEN though she wants to run away from this heart-piercing moment, Mary is fully present to Jesus. She walks in solidarity with him and with all her oppressed children. She is the model of the Christian call to be an affirming companion to those struggling for a world liberated from sin, injustice and exploitation.

St. Anthony, may we see in Mary's love a reflection of the love of God, and may we convey healing compassion to others as an instrument of peace.

Fifth Station
Simon Helps Jesus Carry His Cross

ONCE again Jesus is encouraged by the helping hand of another human being. We recall our Lord's words that care shown to others, even strangers, is care shown to Christ. In his life, Jesus walked with people, seeking to liberate them from sin and sickness, and protected the defenseless.

St. Anthony, inspire us to ease the pain of Jesus today by assisting him in sharing the burdens of our afflicted brothers and sisters.

Sixth Station
Veronica Wipes the Face of Jesus

VERONICA disregards public opinion. She will not be intimidated. She rejects standards of this world that see only the rich and glamorous as worthy of attention. In his bloodied face, Jesus imprints on our hearts the intensity of his love for us. We see our Lord's suffering face and Godlike dignity in all those who suffer. We discover him in the faces and struggles of the poor and wherever people are in need.

St. Anthony, teach us through Veronica's example to see God's face in those the world rejects and to show his love at work.

Seventh Station
Jesus Falls the Second Time

THE cross that again crushes Jesus to the ground is truly the burden of our repeated sins. He would not be on his way to a cruel death if the whole human race—from Adam to ourselves—had been more open to God's love. It is we acting contrary to God's will who are responsible for Jesus' suffering and for so much of the human suffering and poverty in this world.

St. Anthony, may we ever be grateful to Jesus for accepting the suffering and pain that took away our sins. May we strive to reform and love with God's grace.

Eighth Station
The Women Weep Over Jesus

THE devoted women who follow Jesus remind us of the courageous role of women throughout times of trial. And Jesus is less concerned about justifying his innocence than about being sensitive to the plight of those who are weeping and their children. He wants all persons to reach their full growth as human beings created after God's image.

St. Anthony, give us an active concern for the welfare of others.

Ninth Station
Jesus Falls the Third Time

 IT is good for us to identify with Jesus' three-time plunge to the ground. We know how hard it is when severe challenges await us. Problems or deep personal loss or failure bring the dark night of the soul. Face down on the ground, we can remember that God's Spirit is in us and, drinking deeply of it, like Jesus we choose to be faithful to the end.

St. Anthony, may we be strengthened by the persevering spirit of Jesus when we feel defeated or tempted to give in.

Tenth Station
Jesus Is Stripped of His Garments

AS if the whipping and crowning with thorns are not enough, Jesus' clothes are now torn from his wounded skin. This irreverence is not simply against his body but against the sacredness, integrity and privacy of his inner person. In a sense he is stripped of every shred of human dignity—like those violated today by torture or sexual exploitation or abuse. Yet he stands before his persecutors with a glory that no one can take away.

St. Anthony, strengthen us to live in truth and honesty before others and God our Creator, who has invested us with enduring dignity.

Eleventh Station
Jesus Is Nailed to the Cross

BECAUSE of Jesus' forgiving heart, he lets the very nails we drive into his hands and feet drive away our guilt. Jesus' love is so pure and generous that he seeks only to build up others, no matter what they do to him. But perhaps Jesus' greatest gift is his forgiveness. For without it, we are alienated from God and from each other. With it, we are set free to be one with God, ourselves and one another.

St. Anthony, help us to be patient and to take those first selfless steps of forgiveness.

Twelfth Station
Jesus Dies on the Cross

AS he hangs dying on the cross, Jesus is tempted, as many are sometimes, to doubt God's presence in his struggle. But in the end he dies the way he has lived—with total trust in his Father's love. Out of the darkness of defeat comes the world's redemption. In each Eucharist, Jesus gives us glimpses of the God-nourished society of love, unity and mutual healing that the whole world is meant to become.

St. Anthony, inspire us to feel God's presence and proclaim by our loving lives that Jesus is the savior of the world.

Thirteenth Station
Jesus Is Taken Down from the Cross

THE lifeless body of Jesus is lowered into Mary's arms. This human shell created by God had contained the most honorable life that ever lived. Jesus has given much: a whole life dedicated to healing people. Standing in awe before this broken body, we affirm that it is God's power and not our human success that accomplishes the coming of the Kingdom.

St. Anthony, help us to empty ourselves of selfishness so that we may imitate the total giving of Jesus.

Fourteenth Station
Jesus Is Laid in the Tomb

THOUGH the embalmed body of Jesus is placed in a tomb, his work is not stopped. In three days God will raise him to new life, and he will go into every place where his mission is to flourish. We are also called to plunge into the mission of the risen Lord and be witnesses of his liberating presence in our world.

St. Anthony, help us continue our Lord's mission of liberating the human family from suffering and injustice that results from sin.

Closing Prayer

LORD Jesus, in your mercy you have given us new birth into hope, which draws its life from your resurrection. By dying, you destroyed our death, and by rising you have restored our life. You are now at work in our hearts through the energy of your Spirit. Strengthened by this power, we will do our best to show your love at work and try to cope patiently and lovingly with life's challenges. We are comforted by our belief that the sufferings of this life cannot be compared to the joys that await us in eternal life. May our Lady of Sorrows walk with us on our way. Amen.

Traditional Prayers

St. Bonaventure's Prayer in Honor of St. Anthony

(When St. Anthony's tomb was opened in 1263, St. Bonaventure, the General Minister of the Franciscan Order, was present and found to his surprise that the Saint's tongue had been preserved intact.)

O blessed tongue! that never ceased to praise God, and taught others to bless him, it is now manifest how precious you are in his sight!

(The remains of St. Anthony underwent a careful scientific examination in January 1981. Among the discoveries was that the entire voice mechanism of the Saint remains intact. His tongue is now reserved in a special reliquary at the Basilica. These relics remind us how St. Anthony so powerfully defended the faith and the poor.)

O Glorious Virgin

(While on his deathbed, June 13, 1231, St. Anthony sang his favorite hymn to the Mother of God, "O Gloriosa Virginum.")

O Glorious Virgin Mary, exalted far above the heavens,
You nursed your Creator as your very own child.

What was sadly lost through Adam and Eve
You have restored through the fruit of your
    womb, Jesus.
You opened the doors of heaven to us
Who cry out from here below.

Through you came heaven's exalted King,
Through you shone the Light of our Salva-
    tion,
Jesus Christ, our Lord.

Give praise all you nations redeemed by
    Christ,
For Jesus, our Life, given through the Virgin
    Mary.

Glory to you, Lord Jesus,
Born of the Virgin Mary,
To the Father and the Life-Giving Spirit,
For age upon age unending. Amen.

The Responsory of St. Anthony

(Composed by Fr. Julian of Spires, a contemporary and confrere of St. Anthony, this hymn of praise was later attributed to St. Bonaventure, probably because he publicized it.)

Leader:
If then you ask for miracles
Death, error, all calamities,
The leprosy and demons fly,
And health succeeds infirmities.

All:
The sea obeys, and fetters break,
And lifeless limbs you do restore.

While treasures lost are found again,
When young and old your aid implore.

Leader:

All dangers vanish at your prayer,
And deepest needs are cared for, too.
Let those who know your power proclaim,
Let Paduans say, "These are of you."

All:

The sea obeys . . . .

Leader:

To Father, Son, may glory be,
And Holy Spirit eternally.

All:

The sea obeys . . . .

Leader:

Pray for us, St. Anthony,

All:

That we may be made worthy of the promises of Christ.

Leader:

God, our loving Father,

All:

You are glorified in your servant St. Anthony,
whose glory is the crowning of your gifts to him.
In his life on earth you give us an example.
In our prayerful communion with him
you give us his friendship.

**In his prayer for the Church
you give us strength and protection.
We praise and thank you, Lord,
for these benefits through Jesus Christ, your
Son.
Amen.**

St. Anthony's Blessing

(A tradition from the 14th century tells of a woman in Lisbon, Portugal, tempted by the devil to take her life. She received in a dream comforting words from St. Anthony, and on awakening discovered a prayer in her hand. She used this prayer, known today as "St. Anthony's Blessing," to overcome temptations. The Church once incorporated this prayer against the powers of evil in its ritual for an exorcism.)

BEHOLD, the Cross of the Lord!
Begone, all evil powers!
The Lion of the tribe of Judah,
The Root of David, has conquered!
Alleluia, Alleluia!

("Lion" and "Root" are messianic titles from The Book of Revelation 5:5. They are applied to Jesus Christ to symbolize his victory over sin and death as our Redeemer.

Litany of St. Anthony

(For private use only)

LORD, have mercy.
Christ, have mercy.
Lord, have mercy.
Christ, hear us
Christ, graciously hear us.
God, the Father of heaven,
have mercy on us.
God, the Son, Redeemer of the world,
have mercy on us.
God, the Holy Spirit,
have mercy on us.
Holy Trinity, one God,
have mercy on us.

Holy Mary, *pray for us*.
Holy Father Francis,*
St. Anthony of Padua,
St. Anthony, glory of the Order of Friars Minor,
St. Anthony, martyr in desiring to die for Christ,
St. Anthony, pillar of the Church,
St. Anthony, devoted priest of God,
St. Anthony, apostolic preacher,
St. Anthony, teacher of truth,
St. Anthony, protector against evil,
St. Anthony, comforter of the troubled,
St. Anthony, helper in our needs,
St. Anthony, deliverer of the hostage,
St. Anthony, guide of the erring,
St. Anthony, finder of lost things,
St. Anthony, chosen intercessor,
St. Anthony, continuous worker of miracles,

St. Anthony, Doctor of the Gospel,
Be merciful to us, *spare us, O Lord.*
Be merciful to us, *hear us, O Lord.*

From all evil, *deliver us, O Lord.*
From all sin,**
From all dangers of body and soul,
From the snares of the devil,
From famine, epidemics, and war,
From eternal death,
Through the merits of St. Anthony,
Through his zeal for the conversion of sinners,
Through his desire for the crown of martyrdom,
Through his fatigues and labors,
Through his preaching and teaching,
Through his penance,
Through his patience and humility,

* "Pray for us" is repeated after every invocation until "St. Anthony, Doctor of the Gospel" inclusive.

** "Deliver us, O Lord" is repeated after every invocation until "In the day of judgment" inclusive.

Through his glorious death,

Through the number of his wonderful deeds,

In the day of judgment,

We sinners,
we implore you, hear us,

That you bring us to true penance,***

That you grant us patience in our trials,

That you assist us in our needs,

That you grant us our petitions,

That you kindle the fire of your love within us,

That you favor us with the protection and intercession of St. Anthony,

Son of God,

Lamb of God, you take away the sins of the world;
spare us, O Lord.

Lamb of God, you take away the sins of the world;
graciously hear us, O Lord.

Lamb of God, you take away the sins of the world;
have mercy on us.

Christ, hear us.
Christ, graciously hear us.

Pray for us, St. Anthony:
That we may be made worthy of the promises of Christ.

LET us pray. Almighty and eternal God, you glorified your faithful Confessor and Doctor, St. Anthony, with the gift of working miracles. Graciously grant that what we seek with confidence through his merits we may surely receive by his intercession. Through Christ our Lord.

℟. *Amen.*

*** "We implore you, hear us" is repeated after every invocation until "Son of God" inclusive.

The Chaplet or Beads of St. Anthony

*I*N *recent times the custom has spread worldwide of praying 13 Our Fathers, Hail Marys and Glories in thanksgiving for the 13 favors mentioned in the Responsory of St. Anthony, as well as for personal favors received through his intercession. This collection of prayers is known as the Chaplet or Beads of St. Anthony.*

To facilitate these prayers, 13 groups of three beads have been arranged similar to the Rosary. On the first bead of each three is prayed the Our Father, on the second bead, the Hail Mary, and on the third, Glory be, etc. The Responsory of St. Anthony is prayed at the end of the Chaplet.

A suggested approach while praying the Chaplet prayers would be to imitate St. Anthony's love for God's Word in the Scriptures. Take a moment to reflect on a few verses from anywhere in the Bible before praying each group of Our Father, Hail Mary and Glory be.

Prayer to St. Anthony

HOLY St. Anthony, gentlest of saints, your love for God and charity for his creatures made you worthy to possess miraculous powers. Miracles awaited your word which you were ever ready to speak for those in trouble. Encouraged by this thought, I implore you to obtain for me *(mention your request)*.

The answer to my prayer may require a miracle. Even so, you are the Saint of Miracles. Gentle and loving St. Anthony, whose heart was ever full of human sympathy, whisper my petition into the ears of the sweet Infant Jesus who loved to be folded in your arms, and the gratitude of my heart will ever be yours.

Prayer in Any Necessity

WE salute you, St. Anthony, lily of purity and glory of Christianity. We rejoice at the favors our Lord has so generously bestowed on you. In humility and confidence we entreat you to help us, for we know that God has given you charity and pity, as well as power.

Behold our distress, our anxiety, our fears concerning our salvation. We ask you by the love you felt toward the amiable little Jesus to tell him now of our wants. One word from you will touch his heart and fill us with joy.

Remember how complete your bliss was as you held him close to you, pressed your cheek to his and listened to his angelic voice. Think of this, and hear us for his wondrous show of love. If we could behold you we would bathe your feet with respectful tears and tell you all we feel, all we fear for our salvation.

But to see you is not granted us. Therefore, we salute you in spirit, O glorious favorite of God, and bow down our guilty heads before you in humble reverence while we raise our hearts full of hope toward heaven and you. For he who so often put himself in your arms will now fill your hands with all we ask of you.

Give us, then, what we desire, angel of wisdom and divine love, and we will speak of your grandeur, thereby to honor and glorify him who so blessed you. Amen.

Prayer to the Infant Jesus in St. Anthony's Arms

S WEET Infant Jesus, you are the best and only hope of afflicted souls. I beseech you, through your immeasurable love and grace, whereby you visited your blessed servant St. Anthony to comfort and embrace him, to come to me at his intercession. Let me taste how sweet your presence is to the souls that trust in you.

Prayer for the Restoration of Things Lost or Stolen

BLESSED St. Anthony, the grace of God has made you a powerful advocate in all necessities and the patron for the restoration of things lost or stolen. To you I turn today with childlike love and heartfelt confidence. How many people you have miraculously aided in the recovery of what was lost.

You were the counselor of the erring, the comforter of the afflicted, the healer of the sick, the raiser of the dead, the deliverer of the captive, the refuge of the afflicted. To you I hasten, blessed St. Anthony. Help me in my present concern *(mention your request)*.

I commend what I have lost to your care in the secure hope that you will restore it to me if this be to the greater glory of God and to my own spiritual benefit. Obtain also for me an active faith, peace of mind, sincere love for others, and an ardent desire for eternal life. Amen.

Petitions to St. Anthony

ST. Anthony, our Patron and our Advocate,
grant us what we ask of you.

St. Anthony, powerful in word and work,
grant us what we ask of you.

St. Anthony, attentive to those who invoke
　　you,
　grant us what we ask of you.

St. Anthony, glory of the Church and honor
　　of the Franciscan Order,
　grant us what we ask of you.

St. Anthony, whom the Infant Jesus so much
　　loved and honored,
　grant us what we ask of you.

An Act of Consecration
to St. Anthony

GLORIOUS St. Anthony, servant and
friend of God, I salute you through the
most loving heart of our Divine Savior Jesus
Christ, whom you bore in your arms in the
form of a child. I choose you today as my patron, advocate and father. I place all my cares
and temptations in your hands. I earnestly
resolve never to forsake you.

Great Saint, obtain for me and all your
other friends perfect purity of body and soul.
I also, in imitation of your zeal, promise to
lead others to the knowledge, the love and
the service of God through my own example
and counsel. Amen.

Prayer of Thanksgiving to St. Anthony

ST. Anthony, glorious Wonder Worker, father of the poor and comforter of the troubled, you have come to my assistance with great kindness and strengthened me abundantly. I come to you to return my heartfelt thanks.

Accept my offering and, with it, my sincere promise, which I now renew, to live always in the love of Jesus and my neighbor. Continue to shield me graciously by your protection, and obtain for me the final grace of being able one day to enter the kingdom of heaven and sing with you the everlasting praises of God. Amen.

Memorare of St. Anthony

REMEMBER, our miracle-working Saint, that it never was heard that you have left without help or relief anyone in need who had recourse to you. With my heart fully confident, I come to you for refuge, most favored and blessed friend of the Infant Jesus. Eloquent preacher of the divine mercies, despise not my prayers, but, bringing them before the throne of God, strengthen them by your intercession and obtain for me what I ask—help and consolation in my needs. Amen.

The Franciscan Crown

(The Rosary of the Seven Joys of the Blessed Virgin)

Although not a devotion to St. Anthony, the Franciscan Crown is included here in testimony to the Saint's devotion to the Mother of Jesus.

A YOUNG novice in the Franciscan Order was favored with an apparition of Mary. She taught him this version of the Rosary.

Make the Sign of the Cross and begin immediately with the first decade, saying one Our Father and 10 Hail Marys. There is no Creed or opening prayers. Continue in the same manner with the remaining six decades, reciting each decade in honor of a joyful event in Mary's life: (1) The Annunciation; (2) The Visitation; (3) The Birth of Jesus; (4) The Adoration of the Magi; (5) The Finding of the Child Jesus in the Temple; (6) The Apparition of the Risen Jesus to his Mother; (7) Mary's Assumption into Heaven and Coronation as Queen.

After the seventh decade, say two final Hail Marys in our Lady's honor.

Contemporary Prayers

St. Anthony, Promoter of Eucharistic Devotion

S T. Anthony, you nourished your love of Christ and the Church through the Bible and the Sacrament of the Altar. Share with me your burning desire to seek Christ in the prayerful study of God's Holy Word and the faithful celebration and reception of Christ in the Sacrament of the Eucharist.

Allow these Sacred Mysteries of Christ's Saving Presence to inspire and strengthen me so that I might live Christ's own life through deeds of self-sacrificing love on behalf of all, especially the poor and unwanted. As a sure help may I approach Mary, the Mother of God, with your childlike confidence for she can lead me to proper worship of Christ and service to him in the Church and the world.

And when my witness to Christ brings trial help me to unite myself to the sufferings of Christ in the sure hope of a share in the Banquet of Eternal Life in heaven with you and all God's Holy Ones. For this I hope, St. Anthony; for this I pray. Amen.

✠ *Bernard Cardinal Law, Archbishop of Boston*

Respect for Nature

DEAR Creator, may St. Anthony, with Brother St. Francis, help us to keep a sense of community with all people and all creation, even Brother Sun, Sister Moon and Mother Earth.

Help us realize that when we are at peace with you and your world, we can invite all to share this peace. Remind us of our obligation to respect all your creation with care. Amen.

Christian Life

GOD, I praise you that St. Anthony always sought to bear witness to Christ in every situation. Help me also to live as a joyful Christian, faithful to the promises of my Baptism. I pray for a willingness to accept your Will and to give myself generously in my calling in life. Allow me to show your love at work in me by sharing what I have with others.

Grant that I may meet temptation with a confidence in Christ's power to strengthen me. Recognizing my imperfections, may I regularly celebrate Reconciliation and receive Christ in Communion, which nourishes his life in me. As St. Anthony did in his way, help me to find you in my way so I may share your friendship. Amen.

Kindness in Speech

L OVING God, may I always use my tongue as St. Anthony did, to praise your hallowed name and make you known among those I meet. Help me to avoid all cursing, lies and unkind words. Give me a tongue to speak in ways that will encourage others and show love for them. Amen.

Purity of Heart

G OD, a pure heart will help make me a clear instrument for your peace. I thank you for the example of St. Anthony's faithful obedience to the holy Gospel.

Give me the grace to accept the challenge of keeping my heart a pure temple for your Holy Spirit. Amen.

Family

G OD our Creator, you blessed St. Anthony with a loving family to help his Christian formation. Bless our family and help us grow together in faith by prayer and open concern for each other.

Strengthen the bonds of love among us through our faithful celebration of the Eucharist, which makes us one in Christ. We thank you, Lord, for our daily bread, so that we may share with all whom we meet the Love and Mystery of Christ in human life.

Protect our children and young people in their years of growth and development. Help them to be pure in heart and faithful to good relationships.

Stand by those members of our family in advanced years. Grant them the comfort of their faith, their family and friends. We surrender to you our departed loved ones, knowing that we will be united in your eternal kingdom. Amen.

Children

L ORD God, you love the innocence and goodness of children. May their parents guide them in faith and wisdom and protect them from evil. Bless my own little ones and keep them in your tender care. May all children experience the near presence of St. Anthony watching over them with his protection. Amen.

Teenagers/Young Adults

S T. Anthony, friend of all, I share with you my aspirations and desires. Help me to be constant in my Christian commitment. Make me pure in heart. Give me the strength and courage to realize my worthy ideals.

May my studies and work prepare me for life so that I may help anyone who may be in need. Help me recognize true friends; keep me from all bodily and spiritual harm. Make me firm in my convictions. Amen

Studies

ALL-knowing God, you blessed St. Anthony with human and Christian wisdom.

You know how important my studies are for my life and the commitment they require of me. I pray for a firm will to apply myself to this commitment.

May school be for me an arena of life where I may apply to human knowledge the teachings of my faith. May I continue my studies successfully and be useful to others with Christian responsibility. Amen.

Choice of a Happy State in Life

GUIDING Lord, you enlightened St. Anthony to know the calling in life where he attained a high degree of holiness. May I also receive the grace to recognize and embrace situations in life to which I am called.

Help me bloom where I am planted. Amen.

Peace of Mind

LOVING God, I praise you for the faith that St. Anthony had in the resurrection of Christ and the comfort this brought him in times of trial. Help my faith so that I may find and preserve peace of mind in my present situation.

Let me discern good from evil, truth from error, so that I may remain faithful to Christ. Give me confidence in your healing grace in myself and in all my relationships. Amen.

In Time of Sickness

GOD, you reached out to the sick and suffering through the compassionate heart of St. Anthony. We ask you to allow him to accompany us as we face this illness and all its uncertainties. Let us experience the power of faith through St. Anthony's prayers as well as our own.

If we must suffer, help us to unite ourselves to the Cross of Christ, so we can bring spiritual benefit to ourselves and others. May the bearing of our cross on earth lead us to the eternal joys of heaven. Amen.

Healing

GOD of Peace and Harmony, I praise you for giving St. Anthony the gift of healing power. Look on me with kindness as I come to you in my need. I pray for healing for myself and for those whom I love. We need healing in body, but especially in spirit.

We need a spirit of love and forgiveness, of openness to God's grace, to help us overcome whatever hinders our growth. Amen.

Return to Faith

MERCIFUL God, you sent St. Anthony on a mission of mercy to those who had fallen away from the Faith. I give you my concern for one dear to me who is not now among our believing community.

Help this loved one to take a look at his/her spiritual heritage and to come to joyful friendship with God. Give me patience and help me to be a true example of faith. Amen.

Freedom from Violence

KIND and Gentle God, I recognize that I live in a world not much different from the one in which St. Anthony lived, where violence and hatred are so often seen instead of love. I sometimes find it hard myself to forgive my enemies, to turn the other cheek.

I pray through the intercession of St. Anthony the Peacemaker that I may be an instrument of peace in my relations with others. Help me to express a reverence for the sacredness of human life in my sisters and brothers. Amen.

Those Growing Old

EVERLASTING God, I praise you for the unique life of St. Anthony and the many thousands of people he influenced. I thank you for the opportunity of touching so many in my own life.

As precious years pass before me, I pray for the vision to count my blessings. Keep me thoughtful of others, pleasant in speech, kind in all my actions.

If age slows me down and sickness comes, allow me to be patient with myself and thankful for the help of others. If I am feeling alone, may I have before my eyes the Cross of Jesus, which promises comforting strength in my trials.

Whatever comes, grant me the gift of peace of mind. After years of faithfulness to you, my loving Creator, may I look forward to the joys in the kingdom of heaven. Amen.

A Happy Death

MY God and my All, I believe that Sister Death will welcome me at my final hour to enjoy forever all the sweetness and delights of your Kingdom.

Help me to die with a loving song in my heart, like your faithful servants St. Francis and St. Anthony. And until then, help me live each day with faith and praise. Amen.

NOVENAS
TO
ST. ANTHONY

*"What we savor through contemplation of
God is transformed into the fire of love for
our neighbor, and thus our face shines like
the sun."* —Sermons of St. Anthony

How to Make a Novena to St. Anthony

THE word "novena" comes from the Latin for "nine each," referring to prayers over a nine-day period. The word is also loosely used to refer to any consecutive span of prayer.

● To make a Novena to ask St. Anthony's intercession on your behalf, simply offer prayers to him over a consecutive period such as nine or 13 Tuesdays. Praying before an image of St. Anthony may foster your devotion, though it is not essential.

● If possible, receive the Sacrament of Reconciliation sometime during this period. Also try to participate in Mass on each Tuesday and receive Holy Communion if you can. Your Novena is meant to deepen your devotion to Jesus.

● Try to imitate the virtues of St. Anthony in some special way on each Tuesday, for example, by reading from the Bible and performing some kindness.

● Try to promise a gift to St. Anthony of "Bread for the Poor" in thanks for favors received from God.

● At the end of your Novena to St. Anthony, entrust whatever intentions you have to God's will. Remember that God, in his love, may have his own way of answering your prayers.

Novena to St. Anthony

(Any or all of these prayers may be used for a personal Novena to St. Anthony.)

Opening

(A hymn may be sung, especially one appropriate to the season of the Church year. The Leader invites all to pray.)

Leader:
In the name of the Father, and of the Son and of the Holy Spirit.

All:
Amen.

Leader:
Let us pray to God our Creator, the source and author of all holiness, who has given us salvation in Christ.

All:
Lord, hear our prayer as we honor you in St. Anthony.

Leader:
Guide our world leaders to seek the way of peace and assist our brothers and sisters who are oppressed.

All:

Lord, hear our prayer as we honor you in St. Anthony.

Leader:

Look with kindness on those who have not had the Gospel shown to them or who have lost their way.

All:

Lord, hear our prayer as we honor you in St. Anthony.

Leader:

Help those who are poor, who have no food or homes, who seek work.

All:

Lord, hear our prayer as we honor you in St. Anthony.

Leader:

Heal the sick and depressed. Let the lonely know the comfort of your love. Assist all in need of your mercy.

All:

Lord, hear our prayer as we honor you in St. Anthony.

Leader:

Grant that our sisters and brothers who have died and now rest in peace may share in your eternal life. Comfort us who remain in this life and who mourn their passing.

All:

Lord, hear our prayer as we honor you in St. Anthony.

St. Anthony's Prayer

(Sermons, II/168)

Leader:

Lord Jesus,

All:

**Bind us to you and to our neighbor with love.
May our hearts not be turned away from
   you.
May our souls not be deceived
nor our talents or minds enticed
by allurements of error
so that we may never distance ourselves
from your love.
Thus may we love our neighbor as ourselves
with strength, wisdom and gentleness.
With your help, you who are blessed
throughout all ages. Amen.**

Scripture Reading

(At the option of the Leader. A homily or period of silent reflection may follow. Special readings for the Nine Tuesdays are found on page 98. Special readings for the Thirteen Tuesdays, on page 87.

The Responsory of St. Anthony.

Leader:

If then you ask for miracles
Death, error, all calamities,
The leprosy and demons fly,
And health succeeds infirmities.

All:

**The sea obeys, and fetters break,
And lifeless limbs you do restore.
While treasures lost are found again,
When young and old your aid implore.**

Leader:

All dangers vanish at your prayer,
And deepest needs are cared for, too.
Let those who know your power proclaim,
Let Paduans say, "These are of you."

All:

The sea obeys . . . .

Leader:

To Father, Son, may glory be,
And Holy Spirit eternally.

All:

The sea obeys . . . .

Leader:

Pray for us, St. Anthony,

All:

That we may be made worthy of the promises of Christ.

Leader:

God, our loving Father.

All:

**You are glorified in your servant St. Anthony, whose glory is the crowning of your gifts to him.
In his life on earth you give us an example.**

In our prayerful communion with him
you give us his friendship.
In his prayer for the Church
you give us strength and protection.
We praise and thank you, Lord,
for these benefits through Jesus Christ, your
    Son.
Amen.

Novena Prayer of Petition

Leader:

Holy St. Anthony,

All:

You are the consolation of so many people.
We come to invoke your help,
confident of experiencing your goodness
    and power.
Pray for us to the Father of mercies,
that we may obtain the graces we need
for ourselves and for our loved ones.

(Pause for Personal Petitions)

Leader:

True follower of St. Francis,

All:

Put into our hearts the flame of your love
that we may love our merciful Father in
    heaven
and our neighbors as ourselves.

**Pray that we may fulfill the will of God
and live the way Jesus shows us in the Gospel.
Be a guide for us this day
that we may recognize the opportunities
God gives us to be helping and caring.
Assist us in keeping the promises
we made at our Baptism.
Help us to obtain the grace
to walk in the light of faith
and to proclaim that faith by the way we live.
Amen.**

Leader:

St. Anthony, light of the Church, lover of God's Law and Doctor of the Gospel,

All:

Pray for us to the Son of God.

Leader:

Let us pray to the Father in the words that Jesus taught us.

All:

**Our Father, who art in heaven,
hallowed be thy name;
thy kingdom come;
thy will be done on earth as it is in heaven.
Give us this day our daily bread;
and forgive us our trespasses
as we forgive those who trespass against us;
and lead us not into temptation,
but deliver us from evil.
Amen.**

Closing Prayer of Thanksgiving

Leader:

Let us pray.

All:

We thank you, Father, for giving us St. Anthony,
who lived the Gospel life so faithfully.
Through his intercession
may the Good News of Christ inspire us
to build up your Kingdom
and make the world a more fitting place
for all to live.
With St. Anthony we praise and bless you,
Father, Son and Holy Spirit,
forever and ever. Amen.

Final Blessing

(The Leader may bless the community with a relic of St. Anthony and offer it for veneration.)

Leader:

Bow your heads and ask for God's blessing.
May the Lord bless you and keep you!
May the Lord let his face shine upon you
    and have mercy on you!
May the Lord look upon you with kindness
    and give you his peace!
May the Lord bless you:
    the Father, Son and Holy Spirit.

All:

Amen.

Readings for "Thirteen Tuesdays"

*(The practice of praying on the Thirteen Tuesdays be-
fore the feast of St. Anthony begins on a Tuesday
about the middle of March and ends on the Tuesday
before June 13th. Use the Novena Prayers to St.
Anthony on page 80. In place of the reading on page
82, substitute for the respective Tuesday the following
passages from Scripture and the Sermons of St.
Anthony. Follow the same procedure for a personal
novena.)*

First Tuesday: Finding Quiet Time

Scripture Reading:

JESUS said, "But when you pray, go to
your inner room, close the door, and pray
to your Father in secret. And your Father
who sees in secret will repay you" (Matthew
6:6).

St. Anthony's Wisdom:

ALAS, how many disturbing thoughts go
through our heart! As a result, we lack
the leisure to enjoy the bread of heavenly delights and to taste the joys of interior contemplation. For that reason the good Master invites us: "Come apart from the restless
throng into a desert place, into solitude of
mind and body." When we withdraw from

the turbulence of the world and rest in quiet and solitude, then does the Lord make himself known to us.

Second Tuesday: A Spirit of Prayer

Scripture Reading:

PERSEVERE in prayer, being watchful in it with thanksgiving (Colossians 4:2).

St. Anthony's Wisdom:

WE can pray in a threefold way: with our hearts, with our mouth, with our hands. Of the first the wise man Sirach says: "The prayer of the humble pierces the clouds" and reaches the home of God. Of the second the psalmist cries: "May my prayer come unto you." Of the third the apostle exhorts us: "Pray constantly," in the sense that the person does not cease to pray who does not cease to do good.

Third Tuesday: Spirit of Renewal

Scripture Reading:

JESUS said, "And I will ask the Father, and he will give you another Advocate to be with you always, the Spirit of truth, which the world cannot accept, because it neither sees nor knows it. But you will know it, because it remains with you, and will be in you" (John 14:16-17).

St. Anthony's Wisdom:

SO, too, does the Holy Spirit pervade all things by his power, for he is ineffable in his might. When he enters a soul he fills it with his fire and lets it enkindle others. All things that draw near him feel his renewing warmth. He leads all hearts upward to heaven.

Fourth Tuesday: Sorrow for Sin

Scripture Reading:

FOR I acknowledge my offense, and my sin is before me always: "Against you only have I sinned, and done what is evil in your sight."... Behold, you are pleased with sincerity of heart, and in my inmost being you teach me wisdom (Psalm 51).

St. Anthony's Wisdom:

WHEN the soul does penance, it awakes and arises. Awake, then, by contrition; awake by confession. Put on the strength of perseverance to the end, put on the glorious garments of love for God and neighbor. In this way you will be the city of the Holy Spirit.

Fifth Tuesday: Forgiveness of Sin

Scripture Reading:

WHEN Jesus saw their faith, he said . . . , "Courage, child, your sins are forgiven." . . . When the crowds saw this they were struck with awe and glorified God who had given such authority to human beings (Matthew 9:2, 8).

St. Anthony's Wisdom:

GOD works the same thing every day in the soul of sinners through the function of the priest. The priest stretches out his hand when he prays to the Lord for sinners and shares their suffering. He touches them when he comforts sinners and promises them pardon. He wills to make them clean when he absolves them from their sin.

Sixth Tuesday: Living Faith

Scripture Reading:

THEN Jesus said to his disciples, "Whoever wishes to come after me must deny himself, take up his cross and follow me" (Matthew 16:24).

St. Anthony's Wisdom:

FAITH without love is empty. To believe in God is to love by believing, to go to him by believing, to cling to him and be numbered among his members by believing. By this kind of faith, the sinful person is justified. Where such faith is found, there is confidence in God's mercy, there is forgiveness of sin.

Seventh Tuesday: A Grateful Heart

Scripture Reading:

AND one of the lepers, realizing he had been healed, returned, glorifying God in a loud voice; and he fell at the feet of Jesus and thanked him. He was a Samaritan (Luke 17:15-16).

St. Anthony's Wisdom:

THE Samaritan thanked Jesus for making him clean of his leprosy. And the Lord commended him for it. He asked where the ungrateful ones were, although he well knew. We should thank the Lord for the blessings he has given us. If Job thanked the Lord and praised his name in adversity, we surely can thank God for all the good things he has done for us!

Eighth Tuesday: The Gift of Love

Scripture Reading:

THE love of God has been poured out into our hearts through the holy Spirit that has been given to us (Romans 5:5).

St. Anthony's Wisdom:

BECAUSE we are God's children we should ask him for what we want. To love God is the only thing worthwhile. And we should ask it of our Father that we may love him as his children. If we ask for love, the

Father will give it to us. He will give us himself because he is love itself. The love of God gives grace in the present moment and will give the blessedness of glory in the world to come.

Ninth Tuesday: Our Daily Bread

Scripture Reading:

I AM the living bread that came down from heaven; whoever eats this bread will live forever; and the bread that I will give is my flesh for the life of the world (John 6:51).

St. Anthony's Wisdom:

JESUS Christ feeds us each day with the teachings of the Gospel and the sacraments of the Church. His flesh and blood in the Sacrament of the Altar is our daily food. He gathered us in his arms, spread out wide on the cross, as John says, "to gather together the children of God who were scattered."

Tenth Tuesday: Gospel Living

Scripture Reading:

JESUS said to them in reply, "My mother and my brothers and sisters are those who hear the word of God and act on it" (Luke 8:21).

St. Anthony's Wisdom:

TO say, "Lord, Lord," in the right sense means to believe with our heart, praise God with our lips, and bear witness to him by our deeds. If one of these is lacking, we are not confessing but denying God. If our life belies our belief, it counts nothing to shout God's praises.

Eleventh Tuesday: Christ in the Poor

Scripture Reading:

JESUS said, ". . . Give to the poor, and you will have treasure in heaven. Then come, follow me" (Matthew 19:21).

St. Anthony's Wisdom:

TODAY Christ stands at our door and knocks in the person of the poor. It is Christ that we honor when we give aid, when we give ourselves to those in need. For he tells us plainly: "When you did this to one of the least of my brothers or sisters, you did it to me."

Twelfth Tuesday: Light to the World

Scripture Reading:

JESUS said, "Just so, your light must shine before others, that they may see your good deeds and glorify your heavenly Father" (Matthew 5:16).

St. Anthony's Wisdom:

WHEN a crystal is touched or struck by the rays of the sun, it gives forth brilliant sparks of light. When people of faith are touched by the light of God's grace, they too must give forth sparks of light in their good words and deeds, and so bring God's light to others.

Thirteenth Tuesday: Reward of Eternal Life

Scripture Reading:

BUT store up treasures in heaven, where neither moth nor decay destroys, nor thieves break in and steal. For where your treasure is, there also will your heart be (Matthew 6:20-21).

St. Anthony's Wisdom:

LET us ask the Lord Jesus Christ to pour out on us his grace, that we may ask and receive the fullness of true joy. May he ask the Father for us to grant us true piety, that we may deserve to come to the place of eternal life.

Short Prayers for "Thirteen Tuesdays"

(Select from this book any prayers you wish for your Novena. Close with the respective prayer below.)

First Tuesday

ST. Anthony, you found quiet time to retreat into private communion with God to replenish your life with new strength. Help me in the midst of my busy life to seek the Spirit's guiding presence within my heart.

Second Tuesday

ST. Anthony, you lived in the midst of storm and danger and were exposed to evils, yet you kept a prayerful spirit. Keep me prayerful and surround me by your constant care.

Third Tuesday

ST. Anthony, you were challenged by change and new experiences so many times in the course of your life. Help me not to be afraid of the changes that will take place in my own life and to realize that by dealing with them I will grow in faith.

Fourth Tuesday

ST. Anthony, in your preaching of the Gospel you proclaimed that God forgives sinners and understands our human frailty.

Help me to acknowledge my trespasses against God and act as a compassionate and forgiving person.

Fifth Tuesday

ST. Anthony, you experienced in your ministry as a priest the power of God healing the wounded through your touch. Heal me and my dear ones according to God's will.

Sixth Tuesday

ST. Anthony, you carried out the daily responsibilities of your religious life with attention, care and loving faith. May I dedicate myself in the same spirit of love to the tasks God has given to me in union with Jesus.

Seventh Tuesday

ST. Anthony, you felt grateful for the countless blessings that flowed into your life from the hands of God. May I also gratefully recognize God's presence in the events of my daily life.

Eighth Tuesday

ST. Anthony, you found that the companionship of your Franciscan brothers gave you happiness and support as you spread the Gospel of love at work. May I be loyal and honest with my friends and respect their support.

Ninth Tuesday

S T. Anthony, each day you celebrated the Sacrifice of God's Son, the Living Bread broken and shared in love. May I nurture others by sharing my daily bread unselfishly.

Tenth Tuesday

S T. Anthony, you walked in the footsteps of our Suffering Savior by accepting with love the challenges of life. Help me to live in your Gospel spirit by accepting patiently whatever God permits for my own growth in holiness.

Eleventh Tuesday

S T. Anthony, you brought hope and comfort to the needy and outcast people of your day. Help me to view any problems as opportunities to grow and share myself with those in need.

Twelfth Tuesday

S T. Anthony, you led many from darkness to light by your preaching and works of kindness. May I also become light to others and a radiant instrument of peace.

Thirteenth Tuesday

S T. Anthony, you rejoiced in God's mysterious ways and holy designs for your life here on earth. I thank the Lord for my own unique existence and for the people I alone can influence for good during my lifetime.

Readings for "Nine Tuesdays"

(Read the Bible passage indicated below as the "Scripture Reading" for each Tuesday of a Nine-Day Novena to St. Anthony.)

1st Tuesday — God's Personal Love
Read: Psalm 139:1-18.

2nd Tuesday — God's Care for Us
Read: Luke 12:22-34

3rd Tuesday — God's Mercy
Read: Ephesians 1:4-23.

4th Tuesday — Life in God's Spirit
Read: Romans 8:1-39.

5th Tuesday — Living in Union with Jesus
Read: John 15:1-15.

6th Tuesday — Christian Love
Read: 1 John 4:7-20.

7th Tuesday — The Life of Faith
Read: Hebrews 11:1-40.

8th Tuesday — The Christian Life
Read: Colossians 3:1-17.

9th Tuesday — Living as Jesus Taught
Read: Ephesians 4:17-32.

The Nine Tuesdays before Christmas

(Any or all of the following prayers may be used for a personal Novena to St. Anthony on the Nine Tuesdays before Christmas.)

Introductory Prayers

(An opening hymn may be sung. The Leader invites all to pray.)

Leader:

In the name of the Father, and of the Son and of the Holy Spirit.

All:

Amen.

Leader:

The Lord is coming and with him all his saints. Then there will be endless days.

All:

The Lord is just.
He will award eternal life
to all who have longed for his coming.

Leader:

The Lord is coming and will not delay. He will bring every hidden thing to light and reveal himself to every nation.

All:

The Lord our God comes in strength
and will fill his servants with joy.

Leader:
Lord, your Son will come again.

All:
**We look forward to eternal life
with the Blessed Trinity,
the Virgin Mary,
the Angels,
St. Anthony,
and all the Saints.**

Leader:
Let us pray.

All:
**We thank you, Father,
for St. Anthony's devotion to the Incarnation
   of your Son.
As we prepare to celebrate the feast of
   Christmas,
help us through the intercession of St. Anthony
to let our lives be peaceful and holy at this
   time.
Amen.**

St. Anthony's Prayer

(Sermons II/47)

Leader:
We thank you, Holy Father,

All:
**For in the middle of winter
you made springtime blossom.
During the winter chill**

you have given us a breath of spring:
the birth of your Son, Jesus.
The Virgin has given birth to the Son of God,
like blessed earth consecrated by the Father
himself,
springing forth nourishment for reconciliation.
Amen.

Scripture Reading

*(At the option of the Leader. A homily or period of si-
lent reflection may follow.)*

The Responsory of St. Anthony

Leader:

If then you ask for miracles
Death, error, all calamities,
The leprosy and demons fly,
And health succeeds infirmities.

All:

The sea obeys, and fetters break,
And lifeless limbs you do restore.
While treasures lost are found again,
When young and old your aid implore.

Leader:

All dangers vanish at your prayer,
And deepest needs are cared for, too.
Let those who know your power proclaim,
Let Paduans say, "These are of you."

All:

The sea obeys . . . .

Leader:

To Father, Son, may glory be,
And Holy Spirit eternally.

All:

The sea obeys . . . .

Leader:

Pray for us, St. Anthony,

All:

That we may be made worthy of the promises of Christ.

Leader:

God, our loving Father,

All:

**You are glorified in your servant St. Anthony,
whose glory is the crowning of your gifts to
   him.
In his life on earth you give us an example.
In our prayerful communion with him
you give us his friendship.
In his prayer for the Church
you give us strength and protection.
We praise and thank you, Lord,
for these benefits through Christ, your Son.
Amen.**

Praises of God

Leader:

We give you thanks for revealing your power
in the creation of the universe, and for your
providence in the life of the world.

All:

Lord, hear our prayer
as we honor you in St. Anthony.

Leader:

For the victory of light over darkness, of truth over falsehood, for the knowledge of your prophetic word setting us free from fear and despair, for the growth of your Kingdom of justice and peace, of holiness and love.

All:

Lord, hear our prayer
as we honor you in St. Anthony.

Leader:

For the humble birth of your Son, for his holy life, for his words and miracles, for his redeeming death to gain us your love forever.

All:

Lord, hear our prayer
as we honor you in St. Anthony.

Leader:

For the founding of the universal Church, for the coming of the gifts of your Holy Spirit within our hearts.

All:

Lord, hear our prayer
as we honor you in St. Anthony.

Leader:

For the glory of your Kingdom at the end of time, when you will be all in all.

All:

**Lord hear our prayer
as we honor you in St. Anthony.**

Novena Prayer of Petition

Leader:

Holy St. Anthony,

All:

**You are the consolation of so many people.
We come to invoke your help,
confident of experiencing your goodness
   and power.
Pray for us to the Father of mercies
that we may obtain the graces
we need for ourselves and for our loved
   ones.**

(Pause for Personal Petitions)

Leader:

True follower of St. Francis,

All:

**Put into our hearts the flame of your love
that we may love our merciful Father in
   heaven
and our neighbors as ourselves.
Pray that we may fulfill the will of God
and live the way Jesus shows us in the Gospel.**

**Be a guide for us this day
that we may recognize the opportunities
God gives us to be helping and caring.
Assist us in keeping the promises
we made at our Baptism.
Help us to obtain the grace
to walk in the light of faith
and to proclaim that faith by the way we live.
Amen.**

Leader:

St. Anthony, light of the Church, lover of God's Law and Doctor of the Gospel,

All:

**Pray for us to the Son of God,
whose coming we await.**

Leader:

Let us pray to the Father in the words that Jesus taught us.

All:

**Our Father, who art in heaven,
hallowed be thy name;
thy kingdom come;
thy will be done on earth as it is in heaven.
Give us this day our daily bread;
and forgive us our trespasses
as we forgive those who trespass against us;
and lead us not into temptation,
but deliver us from evil.
Amen.**

Closing Prayer to Mary
by St. Anthony
(Sermons I/163)

Leader:

We beg you, our Lady and our hope,

All:

**You, who are the star of the sea,
illumine your sons and daughters
engulfed in the turbulent sea of life.
Guide us to the safe harbor of forgiveness
so we may successfully complete the journey of our life
with your protection and with the help of
Jesus.
To him whom you carried in your womb
and nourished
be honor and glory throughout all ages.
Amen.**

Final Blessing

*(The Leader may bless the community with a relic of
St. Anthony and offer it for veneration.)*

Leader:

Bow your heads and ask for God's blessing.
May the Lord bless you and keep you!
May the Lord let his face shine upon you
    and have mercy on you!
May the Lord look upon you with kindness
    and give you his peace!
May the Lord bless you:
    the Father, Son and Holy Spirit.

All:

Amen.

LIVING
IN THE SPIRIT
OF ST. ANTHONY

"All our works count for nothing for the eternal if they are not steeped in the balm of charity. Only love for others invites us to the table of eternal life."
                    —*Sermons of St. Anthony*

Seeking Personal Renewal with St. Anthony

Reflect in God's presence on how you would sincerely respond to any of the questions below. If you feel you have been faithful regarding an area, you may wish to thank God for the grace of fidelity in your Christian life. Close by offering the Prayer to St. Anthony at the end of these reflections.

Suggestions: Take a question a day through Advent, Lent—or any time. Use as an examination of conscience to prepare for the Sacrament of Reconciliation. Explore selected questions at a time of retreat.

My Relationship to God

- Do I praise and thank God for his gifts of love?

- Do I seek to have a continual spirit of prayer in my life?

- Do I turn to God in good times and bad, and in times of temptation?

- Have I shown reverence for God in my speech?

- Do I worship God as an active member of the Church?

- Have I taken steps to deepen my understanding of the faith?
- Do I profess my faith and show God's love at work in me?
- Have I elevated things like money, status, etc., to the level of "false gods" in my life?

My Relationship to Others

- Have I given good example by my words and actions showing God's love at work?
- Do I deal honestly with others?
- Have I used or exploited others for my own selfish interests?
- Am I an instrument of peace?
- Am I caring toward my family?
- Do I show fidelity, patience, respect, gratitude to my spouse, children, parents, brothers, sisters, coworkers? To everyone I know?
- Do I have a responsible attitude toward work? And do my personal ethics carry over into my work?
- Do I listen well?
- Am I open to the views and suggestions of others?
- Have I harmed anyone by deceit, misjudgment, or gossip?
- Have my relations to others been faithful?

- Am I guilty of conversation that is hurtful to God or others?

- Have I acted hurtfully toward others or do I feel unforgiving toward them for the ways they have hurt me?

- Have I shown prejudice or discrimination toward others in my thoughts or actions?

- Do I share what God has given me with those in need?

- Am I guilty of taking what rightfully belongs to others?

- Have I injured the life, limb, or reputation of others?

- Have I upheld and protected the right to life at all levels?

- Do I bring the good news of the Gospel to others?

- Do I promote Christian values at all levels of society?

- Do I involve myself in my parish or local community?

- Do I contribute in any way to the endangerment of natural resources?

- Am I concerned about social and political issues in the world I am part of?

My Personal Growth

- Am I open to calls to fuller life prompted by God's Spirit in my heart?

- Do I try to live every day in a spirit of joy?
- Does my life reflect a wholesome spirit of reconciliation and forgiveness?
- Am I too self-centered, self-willed, or selfish?
- Do I complain about the sufferings and trials in my life?
- Do I take time occasionally to explore my motives and overall patterns of how I live my life?
- Have I experienced the personal growth and joy of God's love at work in my life?
- Am I over-involved in activities at the cost of my responsibilities or my own peace?
- Do I need to work on dealing with attitudes like pride, arrogance, or jealousy?
- Do I have a healthy love for myself and appreciate my unique goodness as a person?
- Have I willfully indulged in thoughts, actions, readings, or entertainment contrary to the virtue of purity and the commandments of God?
- Do I make full use of my talents and gifts?
- Are there ways I could venture into untried areas in my life to realize my untapped potential?
- Do I allow myself to get caught up in self-pity or other destructive feelings?

- What are the ways that laziness influences my life?

- Do I need to look at how unrealistic expectations about myself or others may be playing a role in my life?

- Do I take care of my health? Overeat, overdrink, smoke, or take harmful drugs?

- What inclinations and attitudes within me are hindrances to my growth and development in God's eyes?

Prayer to St. Anthony
(after your reflection)

FATHER, you gave St. Anthony the wisdom and grace to live and preach the Gospel of Christ. Help us to live the Gospel life of love at work as he did. Fill our hearts with your love, that we may pursue unselfishly a sincere love of God and neighbor.

May we be sensitive to your call and faithful to our baptismal promises. May we imitate the life and work of St. Anthony and create a new world where the love of Jesus will be the rule and not the exception. We make our prayer through Christ our Lord. Amen.

Affirmations of God's Love in the Spirit of St. Anthony

"Dear brothers and sisters, let us humbly beg Jesus Christ in his loving kindness to come and stand before us, to bestow his peace on us, to take away our sins, to dispel all doubt from our hearts, and to impress on our minds belief in his passion and resurrection.... Let us ask the Lord Jesus Christ to pour out on us his grace that we may ask for and receive the fullness of true joy."

— *Sermons of St. Anthony*

ST. Anthony of Padua spent his lifetime bringing peace and joy to the people of the thirteenth century—and he continues to do so today. The following affirmations are intended to stir up within us that same peace and joy that St. Anthony preached. If we recite these affirmations slowly and repeat them periodically, we will be able to accept in our lives more readily God's love, guidance and protection.

✠ I am God's child again today. I have already been given all I need.

✠ God is with me now. Wherever I go his peace goes with me.

113

✤ God's love sustains me in everything I do.

✤ My teacher, the Holy Spirit, is always within me.

✤ I can do all things in Christ.

✤ I have a mission from God to fulfill.

✤ I am not a victim of the world I see. I am responsible for what I think and feel about it.

✤ I face today confident and unafraid because Jesus is with me.

✤ All my thoughts are powerful. What I think will bring me peace or conflict.

✤ I expect miracles to happen.

✤ I choose love over attack.

✤ God wants me to be happy and enjoy myself.

✤ God takes delight in me.

✤ I see the abundance of God in creation.

✤ God has many surprises for me.

✤ The joy of the Lord is my strength.

✤ I picture only good for myself and others.

✤ I will do only good for myself and others.

✤ I choose to see a world without an enemy.

✤ God will help me heal my mistakes. He will not punish me, so I will not punish myself.

✤ Everything I do and say, I do and say with God.

✤ I forgive by a power not my own, but which is within me.

- ✠ I am an essential part of God's plan.
- ✠ I am enthusiastic about life. My life urge is greater than any negativity in my mind.
- ✠ I will respect all I meet because I see the light of Christ in them.
- ✠ In God I am hopeful that all outcomes will be good.
- ✠ I choose to be grateful, generous and graceful.
- ✠ I choose to give salvation to all I meet.
- ✠ I seek only those things I can share with others.
- ✠ I join with all who come my way for healing.
- ✠ I give this day to God to guide.
- ✠ I walk with gratitude the way of love.
- ✠ Nothing can disturb me. Christ is my peace and my poise.
- ✠ I celebrate my oneness with God.
- ✠ All things work together for good.
- ✠ Only my unforgiving thoughts can hurt me.
- ✠ No one can rob me of my peace, but I can give it away.
- ✠ I am free from tension, stress and strain. I relax completely in God.
- ✠ My worth has already been established by God.
- ✠ God is my help in every need.

A Walk through the Twelve Steps with St. Anthony

(The 12-Step program of Alcoholics Anonymous provides a genuine spirituality, a way of living, that can rescue us from our individual and societal addictions. Inviting St. Anthony to accompany us along the way may strengthen us in our resolves.)

Step 1

St. Anthony, help me to admit that I am powerless over my addiction to (e.g., alcohol, drugs, gambling, overeating, etc.), and that my life has become unmanageable.

Step 2

St. Anthony, help me to believe that a Power greater than myself can restore me to wholeness.

Step 3

St. Anthony, help me make a decision to turn my will and my life over to the care of God as I understand God.

Step 4

St. Anthony, help me to make a searching and fearless moral inventory of myself.

Step 5

St. Anthony, help me to admit to God, to myself and to another human being the exact nature of my wrongs.

Step 6

St. Anthony, help me to become entirely ready to have God remove these defects of character.

Step 7

St. Anthony, help me to humbly ask God to remove my shortcomings.

Step 8

St. Anthony, help me to make a list of all persons I have harmed and become willing to make direct amends to them all.

Step 9

St. Anthony, help me to make direct amends to such people wherever possible, except when to do so would injure them or others.

Step 10

St. Anthony, help me to continue to take personal inventory and, when I am wrong, promptly admit it.

Step 11

St. Anthony, help me to seek through prayer and meditation to improve my conscious contact with God as I understand God, praying only for knowledge of God's will for me and the power to carry it out.

Step 12

St. Anthony, help me, having had a spiritual awakening as a result of these steps, to try to carry this message to other addicted, compulsive people and to practice these principles in all my affairs.

Serenity Prayer

GOD, grant me the Serenity to accept the things I cannot change,
Courage to change the things I can,
and Wisdom to know the difference.

Help me to live one day at a time,
enjoying one moment at a time.

Help me to accept hardships
as the pathway to peace,
Taking as your Son did this world as it is,
Not as I would have it.

Let me trust that you will make all things right
if I surrender to your Will.
May I be reasonably happy in this life
And supremely happy with you forever in the next. Amen.

Chronology of St. Anthony's Life

Anthony becomes ill en route to Morocco and recuperates at Messina	1220-1221
Anthony attends Chapter meeting of Franciscans at Assisi	1221 (May)
Anthony a hermit at Montepaolo near Forli	1221 (June) -1222
Anthony's sermon after ordination ceremony in Forli	1222 (summer)
Anthony's preaching against the Cathars (heretics) in upper Italy	1222-1224
Franciscan final Rule approved by Pope	1223
Anthony appointed teacher of theology by Francis	about 1223
Anthony's preaching against Cathars (or Albigensians) in southern France	1224-1227
Anthony's sermon at the General Chapter of Arles (vision of Francis)	1224 (Sept. 29)
Anthony's sermon at Bourges/conversion of Archbishop Simon de Sully	1225 (Nov. 30)
Death of Francis	1226 (Oct. 3)
Pope Gregory IX	1227-1241
Anthony serves as Provincial of Italian province of Romagna	1227-1230
Anthony begins permanent residence at Padua	1228
Anthony composes Sunday Sermons	about 1228
Canonization of St. Francis at Assisi	1228 (July 16)
Anthony composes Feastday Sermons	1230-1231 (winter)

Anthony preaches before Pope Gregory and Curia and is called "Ark of the Testament"	1230
Anthony preaches sermons in Padua	1231 (Lent)
Anthony fails in appeal to tyrant Ezzelino for clemency to prisoners	1231 (after Lent)
Anthony in hermitage outside Padua at Camposampiero/vision of Child Jesus	1231 (after appeal)
Death of Anthony at Poor Clare monastery of Arcella outside Padua	1231 (June 13)
Canonization of Anthony at Spoleto	1232 (May 30)
Legenda Assidua, first life of St. Anthony, written	1232
St. Anthony's remains transferred to Basilica built in his honor at Padua	1263 (April 8)
Pope Clement XIII and Pope Leo XIII grant indulgences to Franciscan churches for Tuesday devotions	1763, 1894
Pope Leo XIII enriches Thirteen Tuesday devotions in honor of St. Anthony with special indulgences	1898
St. Anthony's Guild founded in Paterson, N.J., by Fr. John Forest Loviner, O.F.M.	1924
Antoniana Solemnia, Apostolic Letter of Pius XI, eulogizes St. Anthony on seventh centenary of death	1931 (Mar. 1)
Exulta, Encyclical Letter of Pope Pius XII, declares St. Anthony Doctor of the Church	1946 (Jan. 16)
Scientific examination of St. Anthony's remains	1981 (Jan. 6)

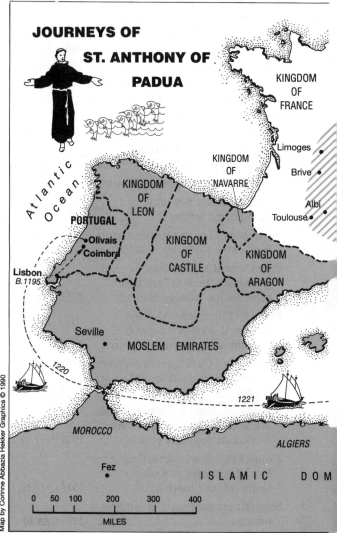

JOURNEYS OF ST. ANTHONY OF PADUA

KINGDOM OF FRANCE

Limoges •

Brive •

Albi •

Toulouse •

KINGDOM OF NAVARRE

Atlantic Ocean

KINGDOM OF LEON

PORTUGAL

• Olivais

• Coimbra

Lisbon
B.1195

KINGDOM OF CASTILE

KINGDOM OF ARAGON

Seville •

MOSLEM EMIRATES

1220

1221

MOROCCO

ALGIERS

Fez •

ISLAMIC DOM

0 50 100   200   300   400

MILES

Map by Corinne Abbazia Hekker Graphics © 1990

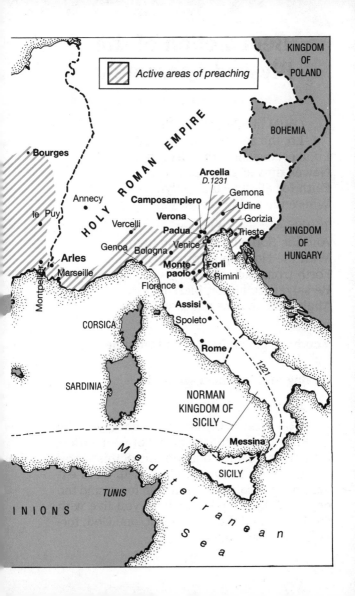

Benediction of the Blessed Sacrament

Down in Adoration Falling

DOWN in adoration falling,
Lo, the sacred Host we hail.
Lo, o'er ancient forms departing,
Newer rites of grace prevail.
Faith for all defects supplying,
Where the feeble senses fail.

To the everlasting Father,
And the Son who reigns on high,
With the Holy Spirit proceeding
Forth from each eternally,
Be salvation, honor, blessing,
Might and endless majesty. Amen.

Leader:

You have given them Bread from heaven,

All:

Having all sweetness within it.

Prayer

LORD Jesus Christ, you gave us the Eucharist as the memorial of your suffering and death. May our worship of this sacrament of your body and blood help us to experience the salvation you won for us and the peace of the Kingdom, where you live with the Father and the Holy Spirit, one God, forever and ever. Amen.

The Divine Praises

BLESSED be God.
Blessed be his Holy Name.
Blessed be Jesus Christ, true God and true man.
Blessed be the Name of Jesus.
Blessed be his most Sacred Heart.
Blessed be his most Precious Blood.
Blessed be Jesus in the most holy Sacrament of the altar.
Blessed be the Holy Spirit, the Paraclete.
Blessed be the great Mother of God, Mary most holy.
Blessed be her holy and Immaculate Conception.
Blessed be her glorious Assumption.
Blessed be the Name of Mary, virgin and mother.
Blessed be St. Joseph, her most chaste spouse.
Blessed be God in his Angels and in his Saints.

Hymn of Thanksgiving

HOLY God, we praise your name.
Lord of all, we bow before you.
All on earth your rule acclaim,
All in heaven above adore you:
Infinite your vast domain,
Everlasting is your name.

Hark, the loud celestial hymn
Angel choirs above are raising.
Cherubim and Seraphim,
In unceasing chorus praising,
Fill the heavens with sweet accord:
Holy, Holy, Holy Lord.

ACKNOWLEDGMENTS

The Editors wish to acknowledge with gratitude the following resources for prayers and other contents as indicated:

Cover: Photograph courtesy of Prov. Pad. F.M.C. Editrice Grafiche Messaggero di S. Antonio, Padova, Italia; Statue in a courtyard on the grounds of the Basilica of St. Anthony in Padua.

He came to You so that You Might Come to Him, by Lothar Hardick, O.F.M., translation by Zachary Hayes, O.F.M. © 1989 by Franciscan Herald Press, 1434 West 51st St., Chicago, IL 60609.

Franciscans at Prayer, edited by the Committee for Franciscan Liturgical Research. © 1982 by Franciscan Publishers, 165 East Pulaski St., Pulaski, WI 54162.

St. Anthony of Padua: Wisdom for Today, by Patrick McCloskey, O.F.M. © 1979 by St. Anthony Messenger Press, 1615 Republic St., Cincinnati, OH 45210.

"The Wisdom of St. Anthony" adapted from *Seek First His Kingdom,* edited by Fr. Livio Poloniato, O.F.M., Conv. © 1988 by Prov. Pad F.M.C. Editrice Grafiche Messaggero di S. Antonio, Padova, Italia.

Let Us Pray with St. Anthony. © 1982 by Prov. Pad. F.M.C. Editrice Grafiche Messaggero di S. Antonio, Padova, Italia.

"Seeking Personal Growth with St. Anthony" adapted from "Examining Your Conscience Today" by George Alliger and Jack Wintz, O.F.M. (CU 0477) © 1977.

"A Journey with St. Anthony along the Way of the Cross" adapted from "The Way of the Cross, A Lenten Devotion for Our Times," by Jack Wintz, O.F.M. (CU0288). © 1988.

"A Walk through the Twelve Steps with St. Anthony" adapted from "Breathing Under Water: A Spirituality of the 12 Steps," by Richard Rohr, O.F.M. (CU 0990). © 1990.

All from *Catholic Update,* St. Anthony Messenger Press, 1615 Republic St., Cincinnati, OH 45210.

"Affirmations of God's Love in the Spirit of St. Anthony" adapted from *An Invitation to Healing* by Fr. Peter McCall, O.F.M. Cap., and Maryanne Lacy. © 1985 by House of Peace, P.O. Box 696, Allerton Ave., Bronx, NY 10469.

Scripture quotations from *The New American Bible,* © 1970 by the Confraternity of Christian Doctrine, Washington, D.C., including the Revised New Testament, © 1986, reproduced herein by license of said Confraternity of Christian Doctrine. All rights reserved.

For their invaluable suggestions, special thanks are expressed to Rose Avato, Judy Ball, Joan Callahan, Fonce Kendrick Forbes, Dorothy and Marian Kamionka, Cornelius Kelly, O.F.M., Dorothy Kinderman, Kevin Mackin, O.F.M., Margaret McDonald, Patricia Ruhnke, Mary Luckey Sharkey, Virginia Waters, FSP., and Vic Winkler.

THE FRANCISCANS AND ST. ANTHONY?

I would like to learn more about the Franciscan way of life. Please send me information on how I can become a follower of St. Francis and St. Clare as a:

☐ Franciscan Friar
(priest or brother)

☐ Franciscan Woman Religious
(active or contemplative)

☐ Secular Franciscan
(open to diocesan priests and lay men and women, married and single)

☐ Secular Institute Member
(open to diocesan priests and single lay men and women)

I would like to help the Franciscans share God's love at work by enrolling in St. Anthony's Guild. Enclosed is a gift of:

☐ $10 for 1 year

☐ $20 for 2 years

☐ other _____
Please make check payable to St. Anthony's Guild.

Your Name _____

Address _____

City _____

State _____ Zip _____

love at work

Mail the above coupon to:
THE FRANCISCANS
ST. ANTHONY'S GUILD
Paterson, New Jersey 07509-2948